The EMPOWERED WOMAN'S Coloring Book

INSPIRING WORDS FOR INSPIRING FEMINISTS

BY LINDSEY BESSER

THIS BOOK BELONGS TO:

_____

INSPIRING
FEMINIST!

HELLO i am Intelligent

hello I am fierce

HELLO I AM STRONG

hello I'm brave

hello i am IMPORTANT

hello i am ambitious

hello I am Confident

hello i am POWERFUL

MAYBE SWEARING WILL HELP

Feminism

Part of being a Feminist is giving other women the freedom to make their own decisions even if you disagree

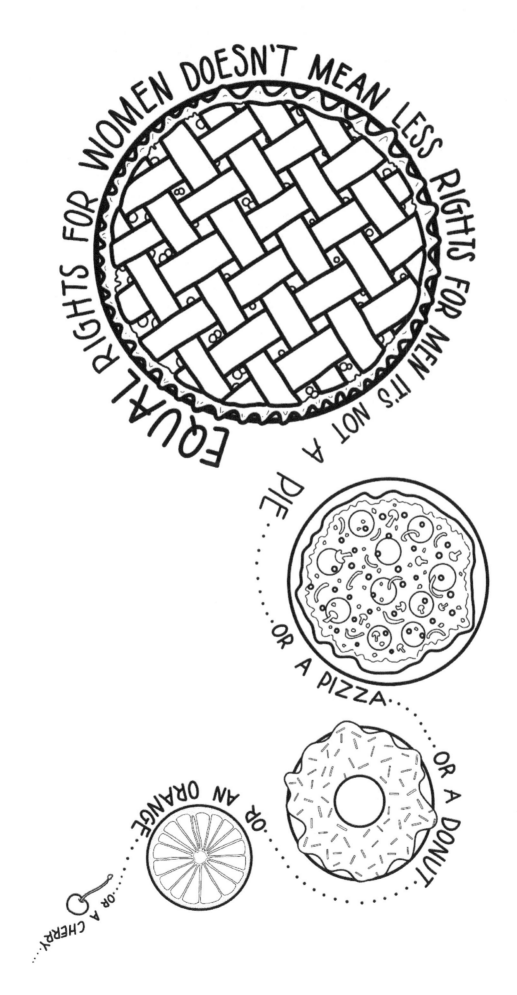

EQUAL RIGHTS FOR WOMEN DOESN'T MEAN LESS RIGHTS FOR MEN IT'S NOT A PIE... OR A PIZZA... OR A DONUT... OR AN ORANGE... OR A CHERRY...

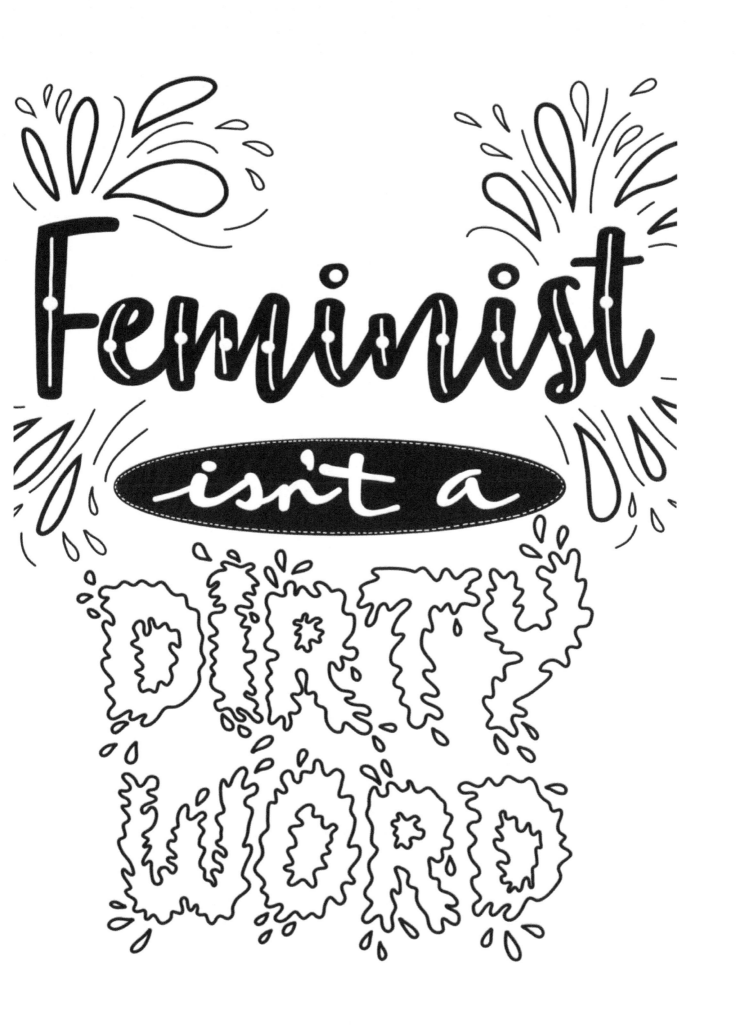

Here's to Strong Women

May we know them

May we raise them

May we be them

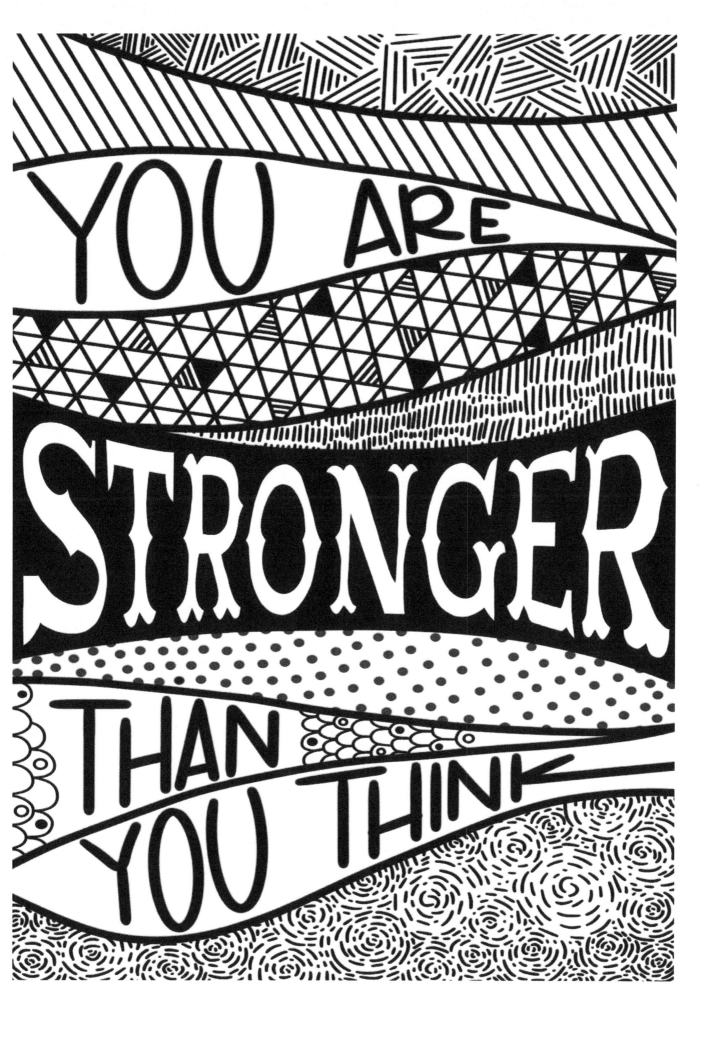

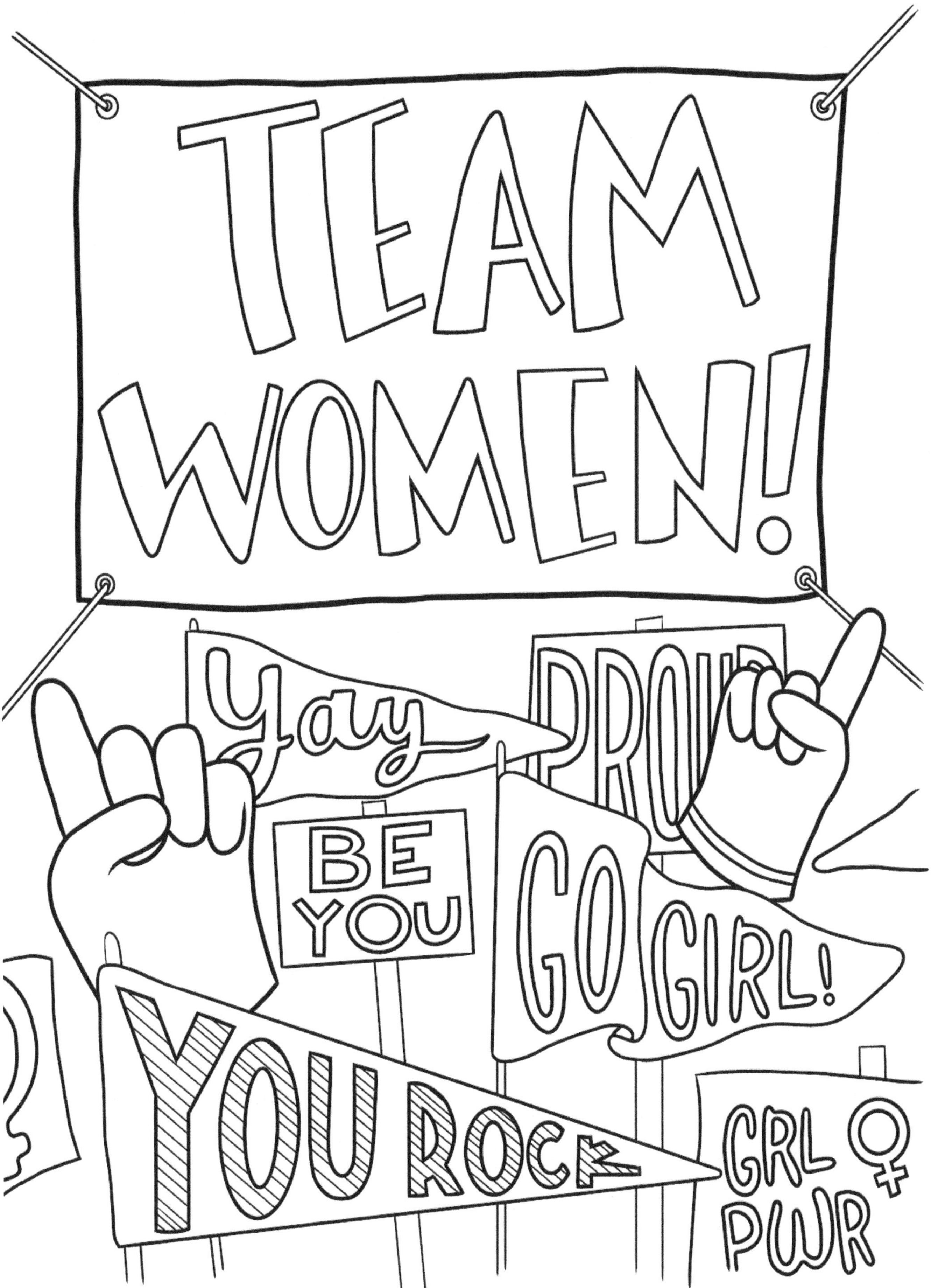
TEAM WOMEN!
Yay
PROUD
BE YOU
GO GIRL!
YOU ROCK
GRL PWR

WHAT'S A
QUEEN
WITHOUT HER KING?
HISTORICALLY
MORE POWERFUL.

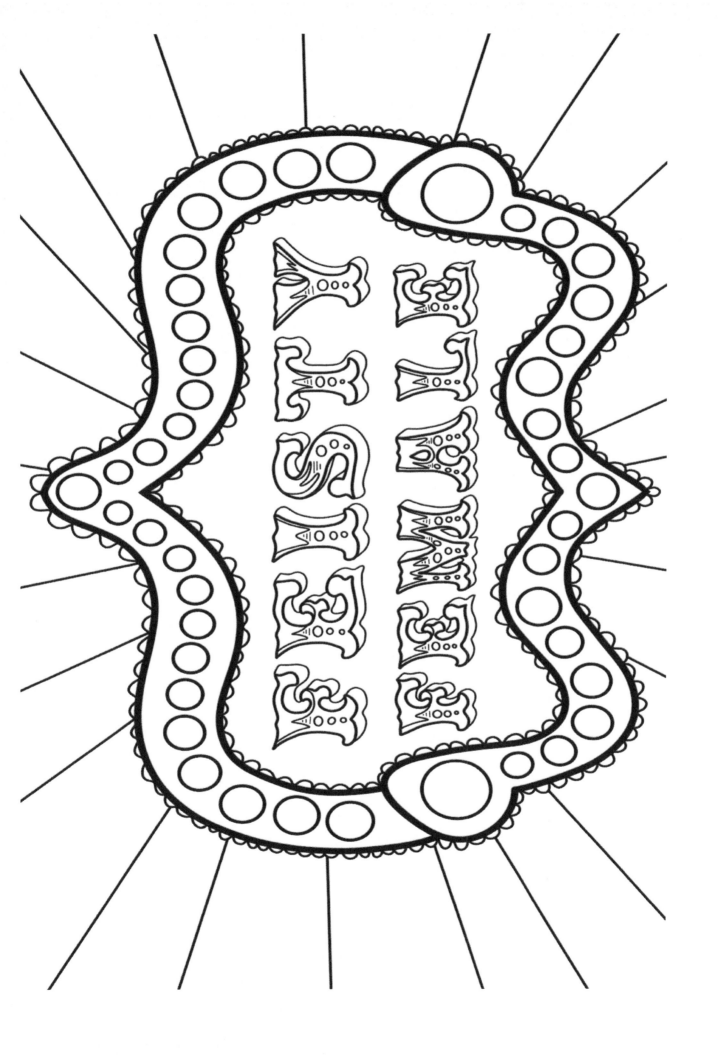

>>> KNOW your POWER NOT your LIMITS

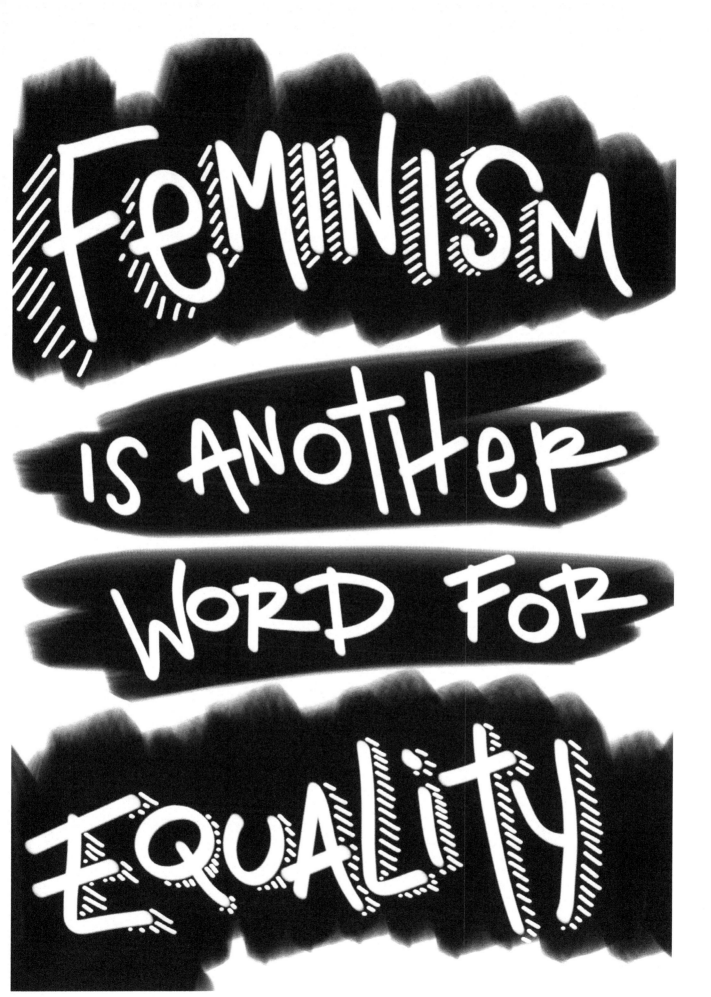

The Empowered Woman's Coloring Book: Inspiring Words for Inspiring Feminists

To avoid bleed-through, place a piece of paper between pages.

Lindsey Besser studio

Made in the USA
Monee, IL
09 November 2020